D1456014

Design in miniature

David Gentleman

Design in miniature

David Gentleman

Watson-Guptill: New York

Manufactured in Great Britain

ISBN 0-8230-1322-7

Library of Congress Catalog Card Number
74-182796

First Printing, 1972

Contents

Introduction

This book is about small things – coins, stamps, small labels and intricate decoration. All of them owe some of their appeal to their small scale; most of the originals of the illustrations shown here measure only an inch or two across. Design in miniature, however, is much more than a simple matter of size or skill or of the designer's ingenuity in being able to work within these confines. An Elizabethan miniature by Hilliard is very different from a life-size portrait reduced to the same small scale, for the size forces the artist to be extremely selective and to be quite ruthless in cutting out the inessentials. This makes for the characteristic intensity and clarity of design in miniature; compression in space giving the same unity as compression of time does in the classical theatre.

Almost everything illustrated here was conceived for print or for production in quantity. Consequently, the small scale of these designs has another important effect, for the production techniques assume an unusual importance. These coins and trade cards, stamps and banknotes all depend on the creative use of the technical means available to the designer at the time, and much of their quality is due to exploiting these possibilities to the full. Many of these techniques have later been superseded by new advances and skills, but the original fitness of the design to the available technique remains as a permanent quality in itself; just as, in an age of supersonic aircraft, the Wright brothers' machine still has a creative perfection of its own which nothing can diminish.

The examples in this book have a second source of interest, in that they all contain opposing forces held in some kind of tension. This tension exists, for example, between the portrait and the inscription on a coin, or between the words and the picture on either a postage stamp or a matchbox; and there is tension, in a banknote design, between the need for graphic clarity and the complicating technical demands of security against forgery. Even in the smallest printers' devices there exist opposing claims between complexity of meaning and simplicity of expression. Furthermore, by their nature, these miniature designs owe quite a lot to another more human kind of tension; between the artist/designer and the printer, or the engraver, or the client. Where production costs are as high in proportion to the artist's own time as they are in the sphere of coins or stamps, these tensions can be quite overbearing; they can act as a complicating or restricting force in the background, and many artists find this too restrictive and inhibiting. At worst they can stifle the creative impulse, but at best (as some of the examples in the book prove) they can evidently provide a valuable stimulus.

Through most of the illustrations that follow run the twin threads of design (letters, typography, abstract shape) on the one hand, and of graphic form or observed reality on the other. These threads do not invariably come from the same source; on a banknote, lettering and numerals, picture, border and decoration may each be the work of different artists; but these twin threads are almost always present in greater or less degree, and they set each other off. I find this particularly interesting because it reflects a personal division of interests present in some measure in each of us – the division between the designer and the artist. This is a conflict between the designer's more introspective, formal, abstract and ordered attitude and the more observant, inquiring, objective attitude to the outside world of the artist. Any work of art reflects these stimulating opposites in varying degrees, but in this book they are more equally divided than usual; and I feel that, although the pressure towards specialization is strong today, it can be resisted, so that both the designing and the observing side of the creative personality can come into play.

Nothing appears here solely because it is small in scale, or because of its curiosity as a feat of craftsmanship, like an engraving of the Lord's Prayer on a pinhead. I have selected the examples on the grounds of personal interest and curiosity, choosing as far as possible things which have been in general use, rather than those which are primarily ornamental or objects of beauty. I have also included some of my own designs for a different reason, because I feel that the practical problems and technical experience they led me into may be interesting enough to pass on, and so justify making space for them here. This gives the postage-stamp section in particular a more personal flavour, and fuller treatment, than might be expected in a book of this scope.

Finally I should like to thank my assistant, Sasha Rowntree, for her care, patience and imagination throughout the work of assembling the book.

9

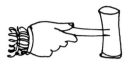

the moneyer's hammer

the pile (the die which strikes the obverse)

obverse face →
the blank
reverse face ↗

the trussel
(the die which strikes
the reverse)

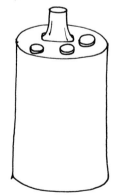

the anvil

Tools used in the making of a coin.

Coins

Coins are both the most ancient form of design in miniature, and the most generally-used today. They are such common objects that one hardly spares them a glance, or pauses to consider whether a coin is well- or ill-designed – or even designed at all. Yet the concentrated interest and liveliness that an ancient coin can afford us, together with its virtual indestructibility, makes it a fascinating and rewarding object. Coins originated in the Aegean about the seventh century BC when the small pieces of gold and silver which had hitherto been used for trading began to be marked with a punch as a convenient substitute for the tedious process of repeatedly weighing them. Ever since then, the essential processes of producing them have remained the same. A heated soft metal blank is struck between two hard dies which impress their images on to it, front and back, at the same moment; the resulting coin would not differ essentially, whether the die was struck by an ancient moneyer's hammer or in a fast modern press. But the processes which *have* changed greatly during this long period are those of making the dies; and even these retained one very important characteristic until recent times, in that the die was engraved by hand to the same size as the finished coin, giving the design an essential vigour and fitness to its own scale. Now, however, dies are reduced by mechanical means from much larger originals, which takes the design out of the hands of the die-engraver and into those of the sculptor – a convenient and practical process, but one in which the important factor of truth to scale has inevitably been lost.

Silver decadrachm *c.* 479 BC with head of Arethusa (enlarged about 6:1).

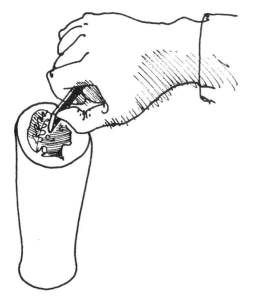

The simplest way to make a die, by engraving into it in intaglio (a concave image).

The earliest dies were made by the artist engraving, or punching, directly into the soft metal of the die. This simple and direct process is reflected in the designs of even the earliest coins, where one can follow the broad direction of the engraver's strokes: one sees them (page 11) on Arethusa's head, running down the nose and along the nostrils and lips, which compels the engraver to formalize and simplify the hair and the conventional wreath. The letters were engraved too, but their terminals and angles were emphasized with a round punch which was used again for the necklace. (The apparently haphazard placing of the letters in reality enhances the wonderful swirling movement of the dolphins round the calm, static head.)

In the infinitely cruder and more brutal technique of the English Middle Ages (left), the same punching technique was used as a kind of visual shorthand, to suggest a face from which all expressiveness has vanished. But three centuries later, in the gold *gros mouton* guelder, we find it again refined into a highly decorative style in which the 'picture' and the surrounding decoration are assembled in a remarkably unified and satisfying whole.

In particular, the repeated pattern suggests the texture and depth of the sheep's fleece in a delightful and vivid fashion; a more realistic technique would have had none of this intensely personal quality, and would hardly have created such an unforgettable image or such a golden sparkle.

English coin of Middle Ages.

Gros mouton guelder. Holland *c.* 1365.

A much later technical development was the engraving, not of the die, but of the punch used for making it: this meant, of course, engraving in relief instead of *incuse*, or in reverse. The silhouette of the head would first be cut mechanically from a sheet of steel, and the details engraved on to it; it was then itself hammered into a soft die, and the surrounding letters were punched in afterwards. One can sometimes recognize this process when the alignment of the letters is not as perfect as their individual form. A good example is Varin's large Louis d'or of 1640 (opposite).

The 'Petition Crown' is by Thomas Simon, the great seventeenth-century English medallist who had also engraved a splendidly severe portrait of Cromwell on the crown piece. It is masterly in the strength of its character-drawing and the grace of the flowing hair, and in the perfect integration of every detail of letter, border, and the conventional costume, even down to Simon's own unobtrusive signature. But, despite its flamboyance, it was a sad story. Simon had been chief engraver to the Mint under Cromwell, but had lost his job when, in 1661, Charles II appointed Jan Roettiers to engrave the new coins in readiness for a new press. Simon therefore engraved this magnificent head of Charles in the hope that he might get his old job back; but to no effect.

Top left:
The silhouette of the head on right cut in sheet steel.
Left:
Thomas Simon's 'Petition' Crown of 1663, with the head of Charles II.
Right:
Varin's Louis d'or of 1640.

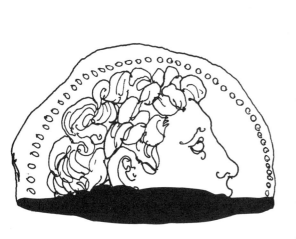

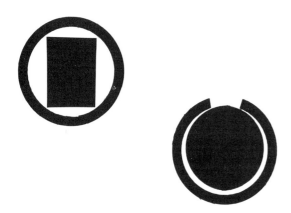

Since it was always the ruler who ultimately controlled the coinage, it was natural that his head should almost always appear on the obverse, and equally natural that these portraits should often be strongly idealized. But not always: sometimes they are notable for their vigorous and piercing honesty. Roman coins in particular show an almost hypnotic intensity in the profiles of their apparently implacable Emperors, in striking contrast to the softer, more poetic heads of the Greeks. Roman forthrightness is emphasized (opposite) by the uncompromising uprightness of the head and neck within the full-circle inscription (weakened only by the little tongue of skin which seems to have been imperfectly cut off). Just how stern Nero's portrait really is, emerges in comparison with the graceful and elegant but infinitely weaker head of Louis XVI. The French artist seems to have shaped the profile to follow the enclosing curves of the inscription, creating an overall air of ease and repose, in which the character or personality of the head seems almost irrelevant.

It is interesting how much production requirements had already altered the modelling of the French coin, so much flatter and thinner in weight than the high relief of the Roman one. This tendency has continued to the present day; solid modelling can even be suggested by the edge of a form whose overall thickness is hardly more than the rest of the coin.

Drawings showing the relative thickness of a Roman coin at the time of Nero and a French eighteenth-century coin. Diagrams to show the relative positions of heads to inscriptions on both these coins.

Top right:
Roman coin with head of Nero.

Right:
French coin with head of Louis XVI.

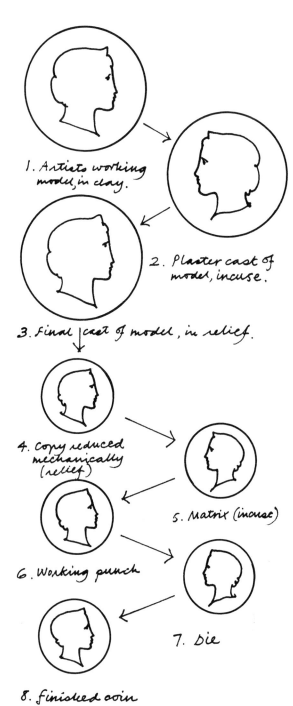

1. Artists working model, in clay.

2. Plaster cast of model, incuse.

3. Final cast of model, in relief.

4. Copy reduced mechanically (relief)

5. Matrix (incuse)

6. Working punch

7. Die

8. Finished coin

In Britain, the commercial expansion of the Industrial Revolution resulted in a need for more coins than the existing plant, powered by horses and manual labour, could possibly provide. After long efforts, in 1797 Matthew Boulton finally induced the government to let him produce a new copper coinage at his own Birmingham mint. There the use of steam power enabled him to produce the big penny and twopenny pieces (below right). These coins, with their thick rims, recessed inscriptions, and total lack of decoration beyond the graceful relief of Britannia herself, were paradoxically a far more radical development than the (politically) revolutionary Louis XVI coin of five years earlier (page 17). This shows how technical processes are more important as agents of change in design than the mere desire for change for its own sake. The English revolutionary coin (above right), with its touching faith in a golden age just about to dawn, is still entirely traditional in technique.

The striking twentieth-century development in coin design has been the practice of mechanically reducing from a large original. The present-day artist or sculptor designing a coin first makes quite a large relief image in fine plaster (6 to 10 inches across). A cast of this is taken, from which in turn an electrotype copy (identical with the first image) is made. This is scanned by a mechanical reducing machine which produces the master punch, a perfect miniature version at whatever scale is needed for the final coin. From this in turn are made, in quantity, matrices, working punches, working dies, and finally the coins themselves.

Above:
English 'Revolutionary' coin.

Right:
English copper twopenny piece, 1797.

Both from the British Museum

19

Merchant-marks

Merchant-marks developed in the late Middle Ages, partly in order to confer a new individuality on the members of trades who had up until then been virtually anonymous, and partly as a convenient trading device or recognition symbol which could be identified by people who could not read. These devices, though they possess certain heraldic qualities, developed in quite a different sphere.

As they were often stamped on bales of wool and other bulky merchandise, they can hardly be classified as design in miniature. They do, however, have a place in this story for they led not only to hall-marks on precious metals but also to the printers' devices. The latter in turn gave way to the modern trade-mark and symbol whose basic characteristic is that it must be suitable for reproduction on a very small scale.

Today, the same need for identity by business and industrial houses is sometimes met in much the same way, by the adoption of a pictorial or geometric device which has to be suitable for use in print, in architecture, on vehicles, and for whatever variants may be necessary. The device opposite was developed for a Swiss banking concern which had three main spheres of activity; hence the reliance on the triple lines and the triangular nature of the symbol, which had to be both simple and distinctive. Once the relative thickness of the strokes to the spaces between them is fixed, and also the 60° angles throughout, a device like this can be drawn up extremely simply and accurately, no matter how large or how small a size may be needed.

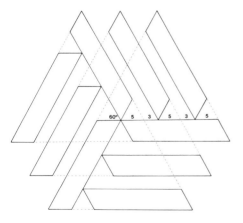

Top left:
English merchant-mark carved on a corner post of
a house in Ipswich.

Left:
Diagram showing construction of the device above
which is a symbol designed for a Swiss bank;
Compagnie Financière et de Crédit.

Symbols and trade-marks

The essence of a symbol is that it is effective at any distance, which means in practice that it must meet the limitations of a very small-scale device which can still be read clearly when it is almost invisible. A remarkable and unlikely symbol designer quite out of his own period was the chemist John Dalton (1766–1844). In the course of developing his (still broadly valid) theory of atomic weights, he designed these atomic symbols. Some rely on an initial letter, but most are highly effective in their use of the simplest graphic elements, and are also easily enough differentiated to be quickly scribbled in a notebook, with no risk of confusion between them.

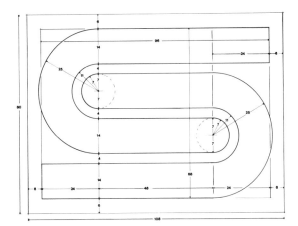

Top:
John Dalton's atomic symbols.

Above:
Diagram showing construction of the symbol for the British Steel Corporation.

Right:
Symbol for the British Steel Corporation.

The problem of designing the British Steel Corporation symbol (shown opposite) was in a way similar: it had to be simple but memorable, and I wanted it to suggest both the strength and flexibility of the substance, and also the corporate structure of a large organization in which individual parts link together in an integrated whole. These considerations made for an abstract, not a realistic approach, which finally took shape as these two geometrical units linking in a shape suggestive of an 'S'. In an exercise like this, having settled on the basic shape, there still remain important decisions about overall shape and weight. This same design could well have been compressed to fill a square, or even extended to a more elongated rectangle; instead, I chose the Golden Mean proportion of $1 : \sqrt{2}$. The thickness of the strokes was dictated by the need for overall solidity but also for clarity at small scale, particularly in reverse.

ALDVS MA·RO·

Printers' devices

The first printers' device to appear in a book was that used by Gutenberg's successors, Fust and Schoeffer. This was in the Mainz Psalter issued on 14 August 1457. It was a semi-heraldic device, the arms on the sinister shield being those of Schoeffer. There is some argument as to whether or not the dexter shield contained the arms of Fust.

The general design was copied and adapted by several other early printers including Gerard Leeu who was working in Gouda from 1477–84. In this case the shields show the arms of the town on one side and the printer's device on the other. Peter de von Breda of Zwolle (1495) also used a similar but slightly more complicated version of the design.

The early Italian presses followed suit and quickly realized the need for a symbol to identify their work. Many of these were severely formal, like the Orb and Cross of Nicolas Jenson (Venice, 1481) – a device shared with minor variations by numerous Italian printers. With no thin black lines to break down in printing, this block would have been almost indestructible in use, and with the extreme simplicity of the orb and cross (a circle and four straight lines) it might equally well have been designed today. Other devices had a more specific allegorical meaning; for instance, Aldus Manutius' motto was *festina lente* (hasten slowly), symbolized by the dolphin for haste and the anchor for immobility. This demanded a more naturalistic approach; (one can formalize an anchor, but not a dolphin). But the device, when cut in wood, was consequently more liable to wear and tear

Top:
Device used by Fust and Schoeffer, 1457–1502.

Above:
Device used by Aldus Manutius, 1502.

Right:
Device used by Nicolas Jenson, Venice 1481.

in use, and had a shorter life, so one finds it re-cut in many slightly different versions, with or without borders. But all retain the same essential simplicity.

Gradually, however, devices grew more complex, like the compasses design of the Antwerp printer Plantin. Finally, they became much smaller. The theme of Plantin's device, work and constancy, was simply expressed by the outer (moving) arm of the compasses for work and the stationary arm for constancy; but a purely ornamental cartouche was added to frame and to decorate the whole, which was made up of the same elements (arcs, angles, and rich realistic decoration) as appear on the architectural façades of the Low Countries of the same period. Another decorative convention was the cloud which forms a convenient 'cuff' for the hand, preventing the need for a surgical-looking section. This reappeared in rougher, less elegant form this side of the Channel in John Stafford's device, in which the stick (or *staff*) is a punning allusion to the name. Henry Brome, another Londoner, printed at the Gun in St Paul's churchyard; his device could hardly be cruder in execution, yet it has a self-confident boldness which is most endearing. But when compared with the elegance of the beribboned phoenix, the English devices are very rough and provincial.

Top left:
Phoenix in simple cartouche.
Middle:
Device used by John Stafford.
Bottom:
Device used by Henry Brome.
Right:
One of the devices used by Christopher Plantin of Antwerp, engraved by Pieter van der Borcht, *c.* 1557.

LABORE ET CONSTANTIA

Printers, like heraldic designers, frequently adopted mythological creatures as supporters for their devices. Philippe Pigouchet was working in Paris from 1483 to 1515. His wild couple are an elegant Northern Renaissance version of the medieval green man, woodwose, or Robin Goodfellow, who had appeared so vividly in the stone capitals of Southwell Minster and was first used as a printer's device at Augsburg in 1477. Perhaps the woodwose represents the earliest form of the ever-recurring dream of the ideal Noble Savage (see page 49). Pigouchet's creatures, however, are idealized even more in their thoughtful and calm expressions, as well as in the controlled elegance of the surrounding forest, very beautifully and lightly suggested despite the unyielding nature of the woodcut technique. The woodwose as later imported into England by Peter Treveris was a much scruffier creature. This device first appeared in *The Grete Herball* in 1526. Woodwose supporters had been granted to the Cornishman, Sir John Treffry (possibly an ancestor of Peter Treveris) who fought with distinction at Poitiers (1356). Perhaps the reason for the woodwoses carrying long bows, with a crossbow (arbalest) placed on the ground between them, was the triumph of the long bow over the crossbow at Agincourt.

Printers' devices largely went out of fashion in the eighteenth century and were only revived to any great extent in the twentieth century by private presses, and publishers began to make use of comparable trade-marks. These varied from the revival of old forms such as the orb and cross of the Officina Bodoni to more decorative or illustrative types of design.

Above:
Device used by Philippe Pigouchet, Paris, *c.* 1500.

Right:
Device used by Peter Treveris. This appeared in *The Grete Herball* in 1526.

PETRVS · TREVERIS

29

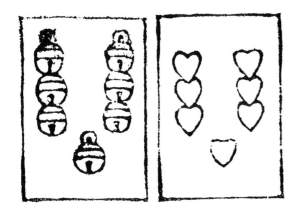

Playing cards

The origins of playing cards are mysterious, but it seems likely that their function has always been a double one of divining the future as well as being used in games of skill and chance. They existed in ancient China, already divided into four suits (coins, strings, myriads, and tens of myriads), and they arrived in Europe in about the thirteenth century, though (being at first hand-painted) they were too expensive a luxury to become very widespread. But by the fifteenth century they were already being printed on paste-board from woodcuts, with the colours stencilled on. Due probably to gamblers' superstitions, their evolution ever since then has been cautious and extremely conservative; the 'court' in English court cards is still that of the Tudors.

The woodcut technique's precision and rigidity contributed much to playing-cards' familiar flat linear pattern; the artist had to cut along both sides of each line before removing the white areas, which demanded great control and produced a very deliberate effect. Stencilling consisted essentially in applying colour by brushing it through holes in a piece of metal or card; this gave a flat colour area with a clear-cut edge, and helped to establish the unreal, formalized convention of playing-card design, which still persists even though the reasons for it have long vanished. The stencilled style appears very clearly in the costume of the card on page 35, and in a more unusual form on the backs of the same pack, which consist of a useful range of questions and answers. Borders and words are both stencilled, through

This page and page 32:
Sixteenth-century German playing cards, using for the different suits acorns, leaves, little bells and hearts.

Right:
Playing card engraved by Jean Genevoy, who was manufacturing at Lyons from 1591–97.
From Le Jeu de Carte, *Jean-Pierre Seguin. Hermann, Paris 1968*

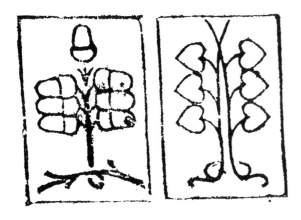

holes which have been made with a set of simple punches; the patterns they build up are as simple and direct as the questions.

Although the basic principle of stencilling has now developed out of all recognition into modern screen-printing, a small amount of work is still done by the traditional process, known by its French name of *pochoir*.

The original European pack of playing cards was the Tarot, whose twenty-two Tarot characters were allegorical figures representing virtues and vices; the Hermit (opposite) from a seventeenth-century Parisian pack, represented age and intellectual isolation.

Cards have always been a tempting source of revenue for the tax collector; in England in 1828 the tax was as high as half-a-crown a pack. The English tax stamp (or receipt) was incorporated in the design of the ace of spades, giving that card its traditionally ornate character; but the French authorities taxed packs of cards by means of a band-seal which, however unwelcome, was at least quite pretty.

Designing a set of playing cards today is a difficult and complex task. The wider range of printing processes now available are not necessarily an improvement on the traditional simple boldness of line and flat colour. The designs must be sufficiently traditional to be recognizable, and yet (if the attempt is worth making at all) they must also break new ground. Several French artists have made the attempt, notably Derain and the decorative designer Jean Picart le Doux.

Right:
The Hermit, from a set of Tarot cards, Paris, seventeenth century.

Stencilled designs on versos of playing cards. Part of set at British Museum.	Right: King of Hearts.

Trade cards and billheads

The eighteenth-century trade card was an informative, discreet advertisement which subtly suggested (or enhanced) the tradesman's standing. Some, like the typeset ones (left), were direct and effective, however unassuming. The honest and down-to-earth approach of John Edwards the collier must have been extremely engaging. The delicate flowered border round Thomas Dugdale's card doesn't quite fit the grisly nature of his trade, and one can't help wondering what kinds of horses he gave *less* money for; but nothing could be more appropriate than the austere starkness of William Marwood's oval or the awful finality of those full stops.

A little higher up the commercial scale, elegance became more important; and the copperplate engraving provided an appropriately lighter and more delicate touch. Trade cards ranged in style from the severely practical, like the tap-maker's billhead, to the grippingly adventurous. The taps or faucets (opposite), were obviously awkward objects to fit into a design, but they were ingeniously saved by the insertion of the Royal Arms. Copperplate engraving permitted new and elegant letterforms like the script (opposite), and also the embellishment of traditional Roman capital letters until they became almost illegible ('King's Patent').

Top left: Eighteenth-century English trade card, printed by letterpress from woodcut and type.
Middle: Eighteenth-century English typographic trade card. *British Museum*
Bottom: Nineteenth-century card used by the official executioner. *British Museum*
Right: Early nineteenth-century engraved billheads.

BY THE

KING'S PATENT,

*New Invented Brass Screw Cocks
that take to Pieces to Clean
and will never Leak.*

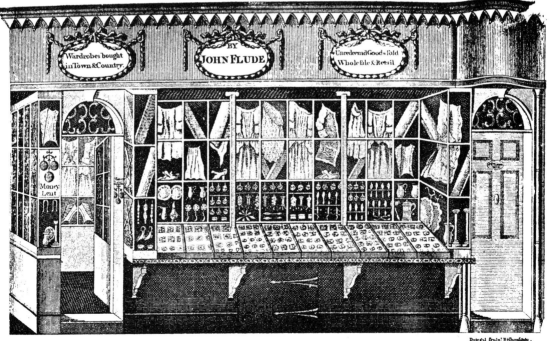

Wardrobes bought
in Town & Country.

BY
JOHN FLUDE

Unredeem'd Goods sold
Whole sale & Retail.

Money
Lent

Deleg.del Sculp.t Bishopsgate.

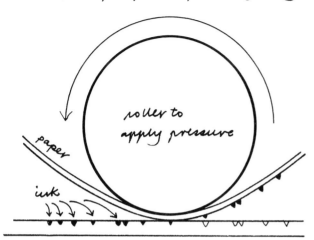

The principle of copperplate engraving

roller to apply pressure

paper

ink

section through engraved plate.

1. Ink is rubbed all over the plate.
2. It is wiped off the surface, but remains in the engraved lines.
3. The roller presses the paper into these lines; when it is peeled away it brings a raised line of ink with it.

Right:
A woodcut trade card for George Worrall, Pinmaker.

Pages 40 and 41:
Two early nineteenth-century trade cards.
British Museum and *John Johnson Collection, New Bodleian Library, Oxford*

The two cards on pages 40 and 41 illustrate the façades of two contrasting buildings. The Blacking Warehouse is extremely plain, austere and forbidding; a cobra-like hoist hovers over the half-open door and the dark windows above only hint at the unimaginable Dickensian gloom of the interior. The card for 'Lillington's Hosiery Glove and London Hat Warehouse' could not present a greater contrast; its well-stocked and light windows are complete with ostrich feathers and a muff, and an attentive shopkeeper inside is helping a family to make a purchase. The lettering on the signboards is airy, flexible, and lightweight. This convention of lettering shown as if painted on the actual building, was widespread; it sometimes existed in reality and sometimes only in the engraver's mind, providing a convenient decorative device for the card, and in this instance a valuable note of solid black.

Woodcut blocks had always been limited to fairly bold lines: anything finer would have disintegrated under the pressure of long-run printing. But in the copperplate engraving process, the merest scratch on the plate would still hold the ink, and the engravers were able to make remarkably fine silvery tones (or to build up a great weight of colour with deep cross-hatched engraving if they chose). They could also develop the swelling and diminishing flourishes round the letters: indeed, the quality, variety, and layout of the engraved letters and script on all these cards is worth a close look. Despite their miniature scale, they have the same grace and careful arrangement as the lettering engraved on the tombstones and monuments of the period.

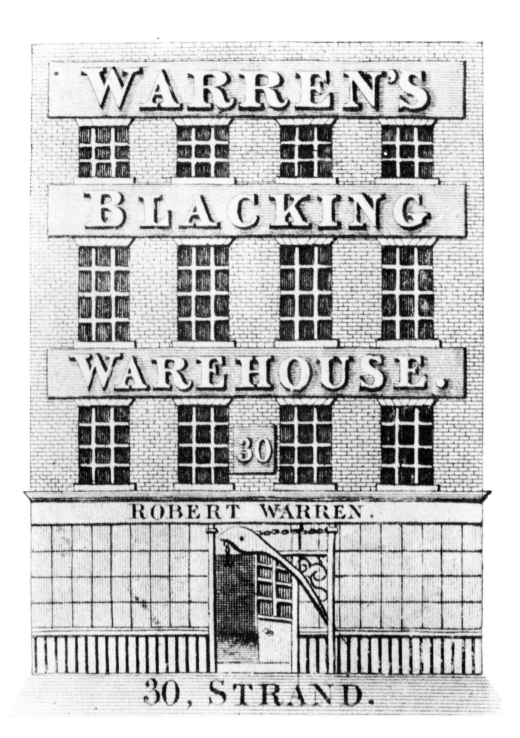

Labels and packs: pins and pills

Once the tradesman had had a card engraved, it was only a short step forward to putting the design directly on to his goods; either on to the paper packaging (though this had not yet acquired the name) or on to a more substantial container. Needles and pins needed to be contained, and their packaging has a long and varied history, from the beautifully-engraved examples of the eighteenth century to a great range of printed processes in the nineteenth: typesetting with unit-border decoration, or tiny boxes with beautifully-detailed pictures engraved on the front, or by contrast the quite severe embossed designs opposite. One of these even included a head of the Queen, whose portrait was appropriated with surprising freedom to lend dignity to commercial products. These designs were coloured and embossed in one process, so avoiding any possible error in register.

Then as now, those products which were hardest to distinguish from their competitors were likely to benefit most from the quality of the package. Animals have always been a great attraction. Overleaf, a lion and a unicorn, escaped from the Royal stable, may be seen lurking in the rococo scrolls of Kirby Beard and Co's pin paper, opposite a skin dresser's equally fanciful vision of a hungry leopard stalking a large but unsuspecting lion protected only by some lightweight copperplate flourishes. In both these splendid designs the intermingling of words and pictures is complete and delightful. Later on, a cunning patent medicine proprietor used a currency engraver to give his pills the illusion of great preciousness.

Above:
Engraved pin packet design *c.* 1820.

Right:
Two needle packets still in use today; the one on the far right enlarged from 27mm high.
John Johnson Collection, New Bodleian Library, Oxford

Two trade cards.

Far left:
Constipation pills – engine-turned.
De La Rue Co Ltd

Left:
French rouge box.
John Johnson Collection, New Bodleian Library, Oxford

Labels and packs: tobacco labels

One shred of tobacco or pinch of snuff being pretty much like another, packaging was (and is) the most important way of identifying both the product and the different brands. This accounts for the care and imagination of the design of these labels. The same, almost mythological, figures occur again and again: the Virginian blackamoor and the plantation, the merchant (generally a heavy smoker) and the sailing-ship. But they are varied of course by extremes of skill and technique on the engraver's part. The cartouches or decorative frames round the the two on the left, have developed from a simple architectural frame (like that round Plantin's device on page 27) into much more fanciful structures which would be hard to analyse clearly, let alone to construct in wood. Bowler's device is still symmetrical, and provides separate clear-cut slots for two pictures plus a title inside and two tobacco plants outside. But on the one below, round the pretty little figure, the foliage and the carving grow on the same (quite asymmetrical) stem, a style taken over half-understood from the Austrian rococo cartouches of Augsburg. This style reappears on the examples on pages 48 and 49; these present a delightful contrast between the eighteenth century's view of European civilization (demurely draped) and the Noble Savage of Virginia, who seems to have shocked the phoenix.

Left:
Engraved tobacco labels.
Right:
Detail of engraved tobacco wrapper, eighteenth century.
Pages 48 and 49:
Two engraved eighteenth-century tobacco labels, enlarged.

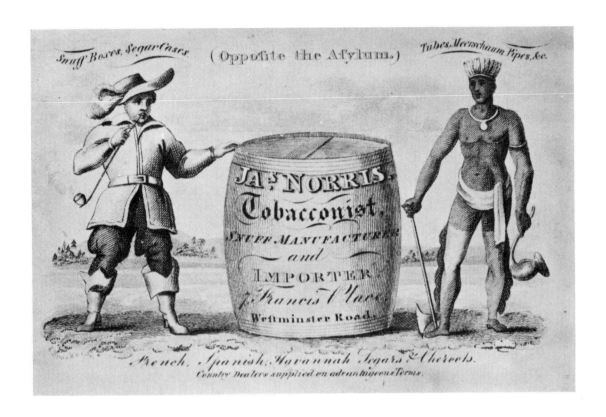

48

49

SMOKE PLAYER'S NAVY CUT, beautifully **Cool and Sweet** Smoking. Ask at all Tobacco Sellers, Stores, &c., and take no other than "PLAYER'S NAVY CUT." Sold ONLY in 1 oz. Packets, 2 oz. Boxes, and 4 oz. Tins, which keep the Tobacco always in fine smoking condition. The genuine bears the Trade Mark, "NOTTINGHAM CASTLE," on every Packet and Tin. Player's Navy Cut CIGARETTES can now be obtained of all leading Tobacconists, Stores, &c., in Packets containing 12.

PUNCH, —OCTOBER 19, 1889.

Labels and packs: cigarettes

The graphic link between tobacco and the sea was to persist. These two variants on a familiar subject are (left) a coloured wood-engraving representing an actual tin and (right) a miniature steel-engraving. The original of this was much smaller, but as the enlargement shows, the power of the steel-engraver to suggest modelling and distance shows up well in the head and in the distant seascape, even on this small scale. The white-line tracery of the devices at each corner was mechanically engraved, or 'engine-turned' (see page 94), an ingenious and characteristic nineteenth-century method of filling-in the awkward triangles left round the life-buoy. There is, however, an air of desperation about the smaller squiggles and whorls which fill in the even smaller remaining spaces.

The letter-forms on these packs have lost the clarity of the earlier engraved lettering, and are just beginning to be more inventive: the word 'cigarettes' in the design (left) is quite flamboyant, but 'Hand Made' is really perverse: look at the turned-out toes of the 'M' in this wretched piece of lettering. Nottingham castle suddenly appears unexpectedly in mid-air, an omen of the pressures to follow in the twentieth century, which tend to the cramming-in of extra detail regardless of the overall effect.

Top left:
Coloured wood-engraving representing a tin of Player's Navy Cut Cigarettes. The design was first used in 1891 and continued in an almost unaltered form until 1962. *John Player and Sons, Nottingham*

Right:
Player's Navy Cut device: enlarged reproduction of engine-turned original. *John Player and Sons, Nottingham*

Labels and packs: cigars and tobacco

Cigars, being more luxurious, needed either a much more ostentatious printed design or, at the other extreme, an absolutely simple and austere device for stamping on to a wooden box. The three designs (left) rely on cautiously decorative letter-forms, carefully chosen to fit the length of the words; in their own simple terms, it would be hard to improve on them. In contrast, the box of Esquisitos is a remarkable example of design-by-loading-to-the-limit: as well as the five (all-different) lines of lettering, it includes an eagle, a globe, three decorated shields, two engraved seals, six medals, a crown, a castle in a cartouche, two sailing-ships on the very edge of a squall, a fortress, a palm-shaded trading-station, an even more distant shore, some lengths of rigidly-folded decorative border-tape, two more flexible bits of lettered ribbon, a sunset, two dangerously sharp-looking corner devices, and a recommendation to 'persons of good taste'. The various decorative conventions (realism, flat pattern and collage) fit together surprisingly well; they make the three chilly mermaids sitting about below look quite subdued by comparison.

Examples like those opposite show how certain conventional styles can remain acceptable and lively in graphic terms even when they have lost their original force.

Left:
Three stamped designs for wooden cigar boxes.
Top right:
Inside packing paper for cigar box, elaborately printed and embossed, twentieth century.
Right:
Tobacco box label printed by chromo-lithography, twentieth century.

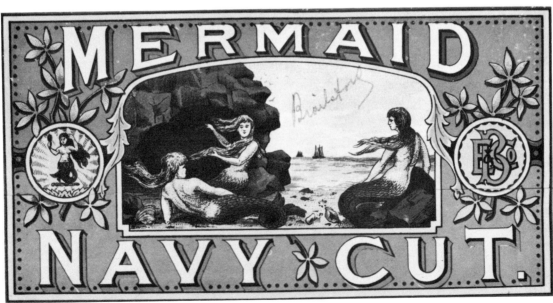

Labels and packs: matchboxes

Matchbox designs, being on small cheap items, vulnerable to the customer's whim, often reflected almost uncannily the attitudes of their age, long before these attitudes could be recognized or analysed. Dixon Son and Evans' 'Discovery' series (opposite) belong to an age of confident achievement, before the dawn of satire and doubt; and so, in a more muted way, does the Captain Webb design, whose hero has been swimming across the English Channel steadily and without flagging ever since 1875. The need to counter the import of foreign matches by leaning heavily on British themes explains these patriotic subjects, embodied in the very title 'England's Glory' with its figure of John Bull. But the tendency was not confined to England. In the 'thirties, the message 'Ein Volk, Ein Reich, Ein Führer' provided not only a more sinister and extreme example of matchbox chauvinism but also a prophetic foretaste of a typographic style which only grew familiar in England much later. The design opposite is a strange and apparently naïve mixture of decorative conventions, from the medieval heraldic echoes of the ribbon at the top, *via* the classical egg-and-dart border round the portrait, to the simple and effective contemporary wood-engraving treatment of Sir Garnett Wolseley's head and uniform.

Top left:
Captain Webb matchbox design, 1875.
Bryant and May Collection

Left:
German Third Reich matchbox design, *c.* 1935.
Right:
Enlarged version of one of Dixon and Evans 'Discovery' series of matchbox labels.
Bryant and May Collection

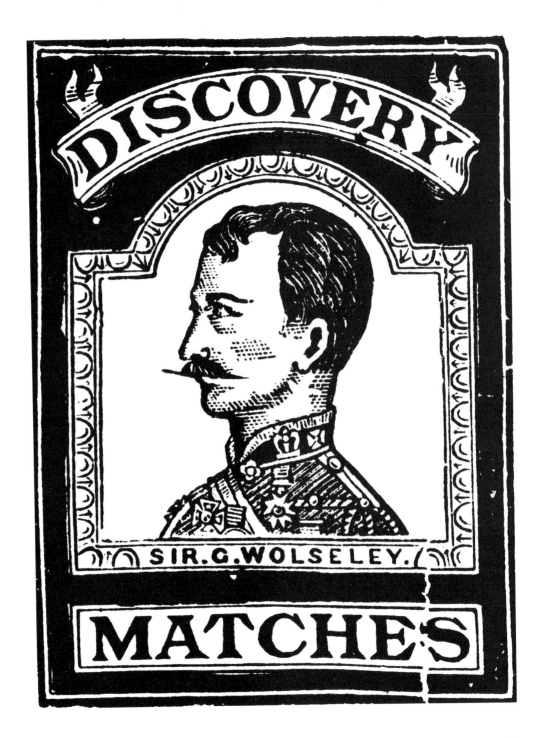

Matchbox labels first appeared in 1829 and every conceivable idea was used to illustrate them. By the middle of the nineteenth century the collection of these often colourful and decorative little pieces of design had become a European craze. The early labels were printed by letterpress with woodcut designs, but soon chromo-lithography was also being used.

Matchboxes provide three surfaces for print, two of which are usually visible at once, so that it is possible to separate picture and name on adjoining panels and still leave the fourth side free for striking the match. The Badger box used identical engravings back and front, with the animal set in an agreeably overgrown scene hedged round with a twiggy border. The tiger, however, appears in two guises; prowling on one side of the box, standing at bay on the other. The letterforms of 'Badger Matches' are worth examining for the amazing perversity with which the designer has decided to force them into two triangles, and the ingenuity of his solution: tendrils sprout unexpectedly from B, R, M and S to fill the awkward spaces.

In due course, the yellow-and-black matchbox became such a familiar object that it was itself represented on the Pygmy series of Swedish boxes, in a highly inventive range of disguises as a Punch-and-Judy show, a sailing-boat, a race-horse, and even a bed. This series came out in 1890.

Above:
Badger matches: wood-engraved designs, *c.* 1870.
Bryant and May Collection

Right:
Bryant and May 'Tiger' matchbox label, *c.* 1900.
Bryant and May Collection

The use of printers' flowers

Decoration by repeating a pattern has existed ever since man first thought of decorating anything. The invention of printing by movable type provided an opportunity for controlled and accurate repetition of the small decorative devices called fleurons or printers' flowers. It was as easy to make up a few lines of flowers as of type, either to provide an agreeable decoration in itself (on a title-page for instance, like Fournier's musical device to the left), or as a frame for a simple type arrangement. The St Helena *ex libris* label is an unassuming example of the latter by a country jobbing printer, made up quite simply from a single ornamental unit.

One of the great advantages of using printers' flowers in miniature typographic design is their value in establishing scale; for instance quite small lettering as on the St Helena label framed in a border of flowers appears to be larger than it actually is. Printers' flowers are cast in a number of different body sizes so it is not difficult to find matching weights for even the smallest pieces of lettering. The perfumier's label by S. Gillé is greatly enriched by the dark classical border, which is in agreeable contrast to the typeface used.

Broadly speaking, the more simple a device, the more startling and effective its transformation into a larger pattern, as one's eye is not distracted by the intricacy of the smaller elements. The *Prié l'Aîné* device, an eighteenth-century French *ex libris* label, has a rococo grace and lightness enhanced by its very simplicity. Without really trying, it suggests a richly decorated panel or frame; yet, if one looks carefully, the individual parts are very simple, even rough, in finish.

Left:
The use of flowers and borders for decoration and in small labels.

Top:
Ex libris label, much enlarged.

Above:
The five units of the border used above.

Watchpapers

Watchpapers were discs, sometimes of thin linen but usually of paper, which were placed inside watches to prevent any dust which might enter through the keyhole from getting into the works. They served both as a reminder of the maker and a record of repairs; and, just as the watch itself was a very intricate piece of workmanship, so the watchpapers were often themselves of great delicacy. 'Time', the universal subject they all have in common, is symbolized in familiar ways: by the busyness of bees, or by Father Time himself (opposite) who (on the belt-*and*-braces principle) holds an hour-glass while he also looks at the clock. He must be checking one against the other. The engraved lettering on the Ripon example on page 62 is remarkable: five different letter-forms in five lines, as well laid out as they would be on a contemporary tombstone. Some watchpapers must have been produced by London engravers and sent out to the provinces, for they are too perfect in design to have been engraved in the small towns they come from. But it is tempting to think that the Snaith watchpaper was engraved by J. Barton himself. (Don't miss the tiny watch which the girl is dangling over the sundial.) Indeed, one of the most invigorating aspects of the eighteenth century was the widespread existence of independent local design skills of a high order, in printing and engraving just as in architecture, quite unconcerned with London and its standards. An outstanding example is the Newcastle engraver Thomas Bewick.

Left:
Three engraved watchpaper designs.
British Museum

Above:
Engraved watchpaper, *c.* 1805 (enlarged).
British Museum

Pages 62 and 63:
Two engraved watchpapers (enlarged).
John Johnson Collection, New Bodleian Library, Oxford

CARTER & SON, WatchMakers JEWELLERS, and Silversmiths RIPON.

Bewick York

J. BARTON,
Watch & Clock Maker
ENGRAVER &c
SNAITH.

Thomas Bewick

Illustrations in printed books were
originally printed from woodcuts and then
from copper-engravings. But early in the
nineteenth century a new technique arose
which (because it could be economically
printed, by the same letterpress process
as the rest of the page of type) quickly
grew to be by far the most common form
of illustration, and then almost as quickly
vanished with the arrival of photographic
reproduction. This development was
wood-engraving: not, one might suppose,
easy to distinguish from woodcut, but
totally different in technique and effect.
Woodcuts had been made on the side
grain of the wood, with a knife;
wood-engravings were made on the end
grain (usually of boxwood) with engraving
tools very much like the metal-engraver's
burins, and consequently with a very
finely-controlled gouging effect instead
of a cutting one. The first major artist in
the medium was Thomas Bewick of
Newcastle upon Tyne, who had been
trained as a metal engraver. It was his
dexterity and imagination in turning his
traditional engraver's skills on to the new
boxwood medium, thus engraving white
lines instead of black, that made his craft
unique.

Bewick worked on far too small a scale
to allow literal realism; but his resulting
mastery of the art of suggestion (of, for
example, the difference in feel between
oak leaves and willow leaves, or of the
silvery glitter of bare winter branches)
was only half his merit. The other was the
faithfulness of his remarkable down-to-
earth vision of his surroundings; he had a
highly *un*romantic view of real life, which

'Tame Duck': wood-engraving by Thomas Bewick, enlarged from 80 mm wide.

Top:
Tail-pieces from Bewick's *Quadrupeds*.

Above:
'Long-legged plover': engraving from Bewick's *Birds*.

Right:
Tail-piece enlarged more than twice up.

was none the less so selective as to be raised to the level of poetic vision. Indeed, he reminds one constantly of his contemporary, the poet John Clare. They shared the same objectivity and minute interest in the natural scene, but Bewick's active trade as an engraver kept him busy and in touch with people, whereas Clare's more isolated circumstances drove him mad.

Certain subjects or themes recur through Bewick's vignettes; the beggars, the crippled, and the blind are a steady presence, as is lashing rain and storm, wintry bareness and snow. One gets an intense vision of the harshness of poverty in the country, all the more convincing because it is understated. But equally numerous are the scenes of shooting and fishing, of well-observed children and vividly-remembered boyhood occasions: tree-climbing, ditch-jumping, making a snowman. If one looks at the engraving of boys who have tied a cooking-pot to a dog's tail, one has to take it on trust that Bewick thought this cruel, for the engraving itself is entirely neutral and objective.

How could Bewick retain this unclouded clarity of vision? Partly by sticking doggedly to his provincial existence: he visited London only twice in his life, didn't like it, and quickly took a collier brig back to Newcastle, so he didn't have to contend with the ambitions and pressures of making his way in London. But essentially it must have been an attitude he was born with, which his active life as a trade engraver only served to enhance. Turning his hand to copper-engraved banknotes and various trivia, as well as to the extended effort of

the large *Birds* and *Quadrupeds* volumes, provided him with the means to exist, without tempting him into extravagance or over-committing himself.

One small but significant difference between Bewick's vignettes and the earlier woodcuts concerns the outline of the block as printed. Early woodcuts are in general cut right up to the edge of the block, so that even where there is no linear border there is still a strong implication of the underlying rectangle of the block, more or less completely filled by the picture. Bewick's engravings on the other hand are much softer in outline, and there is no hint of the squareness of the woodblock extending beyond the feathery edges of his trees or grasses. In this, he is again using the copperplate-engraver's convention, but using it to create something quite new. He was also making full use of the perfect medium for design in miniature. The precision of the burin and the printing possibilities of the boxwood block were just two of the assets of the medium.

A later stage in the use of stock blocks (or stereos) was to cast the smaller designs on type bodies, so that coaches, horses, sailing-ships, locomotives, musical instruments, coats-of-arms etc., could appear on 24, 30 or 36 point bodies. On occasions these smaller designs may well have been cut in metal. They were widely used by the jobbing printers for handbills on both sides of the Atlantic.

Left:
Head- and tail-pieces from *British Birds* by Bewick.
Right:
'The Improved Carthorse': engraving from Bewick's *Quadrupeds*, enlarged from 80 mm wide.

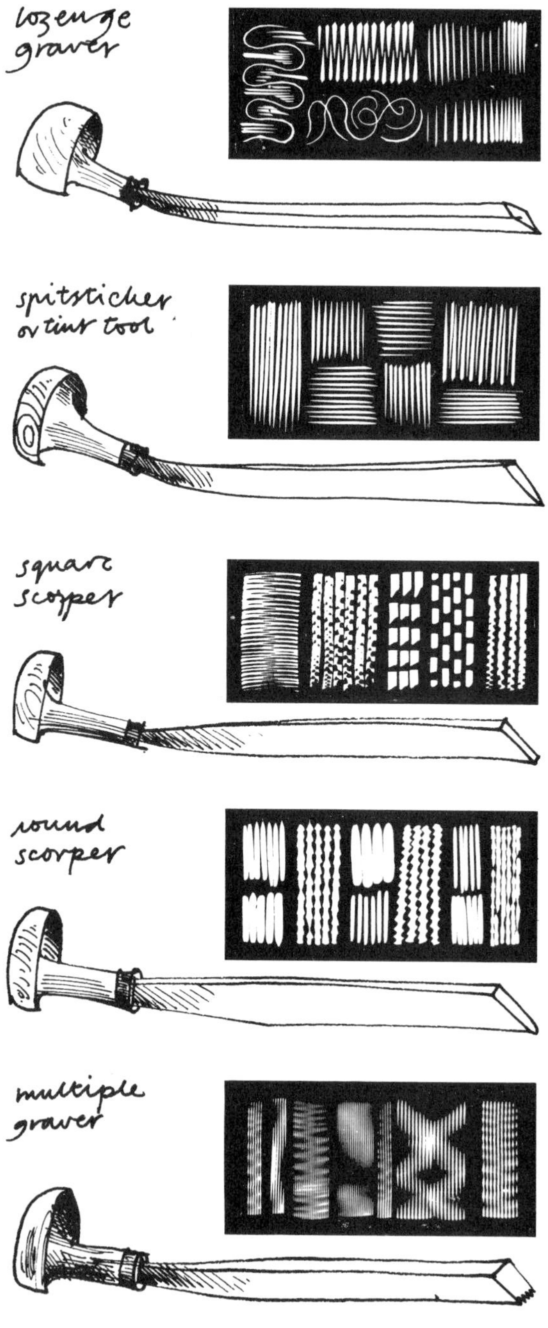
lozenge graver
spitsticker or tint tool
square scorper
round scorper
multiple graver

The tools used in wood-engraving and their marks.

The technique of wood-engraving

The growth of photo-engraving in the later years of the nineteenth century destroyed most of wood-engraving's *raison d'être*, by supplying letterpress blocks made direct from an original without the interpretation (however beautiful or skilful) of the engraver. Wood-engraving's continued existence as a medium has depended on other factors, including the simple pleasure of making a printing surface in its most primitive form. This pleasure is quite intense nowadays at a time when photographic and other technical developments are taking graphic processes more and more out of the artist's hands, or (as many would say) relieving him of those tedious responsibilities.

The engraver's range of five basic tools and the marks they make are shown (left). Each has its special character; the graver is the most flexible, varying from thin line to thick as the tool digs deeper into the wood, and this is the likeliest tool to choose to make an initial outline. I like to work by tracing the design on to a dark-painted block, on which each cut makes a light mark, just as in the final proof: and I often take progressive proofs during the work, to see how it is developing on paper. This enables one to stop while there are still solid black areas, before too much wood is engraved away, for wood-engraving is a one-way only process. If one makes a mistake, however, a small hole can be drilled in the block, filled tightly with a boxwood peg, smoothed down, and the area re-engraved. The progressive proofs (opposite) are for a small engraving for the cover of a stamp booklet for the Post Office.

The stages in a wood-engraving, beginning with a sketch on the block and finishing with the completed engraving.

Wood-engraved colophons

When designing a very small pictorial device, one has to choose between interesting detail and overall shape or silhouette, this last being vital when the device appears as a small blob on a large white area. The Duckworth duck on its own looks unbalanced and it clearly needs a base to give it stability; but if one adds too many reeds, despite the interest of the extra detail, the overall clarity of outline of the bird suffers. There is no short-cut to the right solution. The simplest way is to see how each alternative compares when photographically reduced over the whole range of sizes in which the design may be used, and the final choice may well form unconsciously in one's mind after a period of looking open-mindedly at them all.

The squirrel device (for a publisher of children's books) illustrates another point: the precise difference between an emblem or symbol, and a picture. The first versions of the design, although similar in technique and detail to the final one, proved too pictorial; they might almost have been illustrations. Finally the squirrel was drawn within an imaginary square. This apparently Procrustean ordeal didn't really involve taking much liberty with reality, a squirrel being a furry and pretty flexible creature anyway, but it did give the design a more static and considered 'feel', one which would sit more happily alongside printed type. It also helped the device to fit easily into a square ruled border for certain occasions.

Left:
Variations on a publisher's colophon, for Duckworth.
Right:
The development of another wood-engraved device, for World's Work Ltd.

Postage stamps: the perfect stamp?

The Penny Black was the world's first postage stamp, and it is still one of the most perfect, with its simplicity and its beautiful engraving. Yet the way in which it was designed was far from simple. It involved four different people: a medallist, an artist, and two engravers. The original portrait head, engraved by William Wyon on a medal (left), was softly modelled with great simplicity and dignity. This medal was in turn sketched by Henry Corbould, who had spent his life drawing antique sculpture at the British Museum; he gave Queen Victoria's profile a longer nose and a more classical air. These sketches provided the basis for the final stamp design, engraved on steel by Charles and Frederick Heath; an engraving of quite remarkable beauty and strength.

The engine-turned dark background, with its slight accents of light left between the vertical wave-patterns, provides an admirable contrast to the more freely engraved form of the portrait. (A solid black background could not of course have been printed by line-engraving.)

The final form of the design, though fairly simple, is not absolutely free from trivialities; the devices at the corners (introduced to discourage forgeries) spoil the overall appearance. But the essentially simple conception, of a classic head with a bare minimum of other ingredients, remains a formula which it is hard to improve upon.

Stages in the development of the design of the Penny Black and (opposite) die-proof from the twopence blue.
National Postal Museum

Line-engraving.

Photogravure.

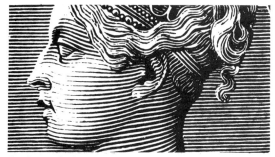

Surface-printing.

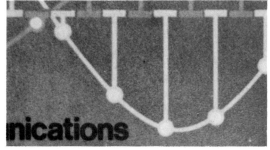

Offset-lithography.

Postage stamps: methods of reproduction

Stamps are so small that problems of reproduction take on an unusual importance. For example, an inaccuracy of a few hundredths of an inch in registering one colour over another, which might be quite unimportant to a larger design, could be ruinous to the appearance of a stamp.

Many stamps are still printed by *line-engraving* (top, and opposite). Where the skill of an active and vital group of engravers is available (as in the US Bureau of Engraving), this can be a very lively and expressive method. It is at its best on simple one- or two-colour designs, and depends traditionally on the quality of the engraver's craftsmanship.

From this method *photogravure* developed, the process used since the 'thirties for most British stamps. Its strong points are good tonal gradation, depth of tone, and an ability to reproduce continuous or photographic tone; its weaknesses are its poor definition (fuzziness) of edges, thin lines, and type.

'*Surface-printing*' is the stamp-collector's name for *letterpress*. It is cheap to print but on this small scale it is clumsy, and it is no longer widely used.

Offset-lithography is in much more general use. This process is good for flat areas of colour and fine linear detail like lettering, numerals and hard-edge designs; but it is not so good for half-tones, where its dotted screen is more obtrusive than photogravure's softer gradations of tone.

Right:
Enlarged photograph of a line-engraved stamp.

Embossing was first used for the earliest British high-value stamp, the shilling green (left), again from Wyon's medal. Quite recently West Germany has issued several attractive embossed stamps.

The first pictorial stamps

The Penny Black was an example of the simplest kind of stamp design, just a portrait head and almost nothing more. It was quite easy to add a decorative framework round the head without spoiling it any more than a frame spoils a picture; this simple formula worked well even in inexpert hands, as in the early Indian design (left). But gradually, as more pictorial or illustrative stamps began to appear, the problems of combining the picture with all the other things grew harder. Various solutions appeared, some more or less successful; the first Canadian stamp, the Beaver (opposite), is a good example of one which worked, for the animal makes a bold silhouette which can stand up to the boldly-lettered ellipse and even to the regalia. All the same, the corners have already become places to put needlessly repeated numerals. It is quite surprising how many different things have been squeezed on to this stamp, and how ingeniously they have been juggled into place; but after all, Sir Sandford Fleming (who designed it) was more famous for engineering than for graphic design.

Top:
Embossing.

Left:
The framed head.

Right:
The first Canadian stamp and its elements.

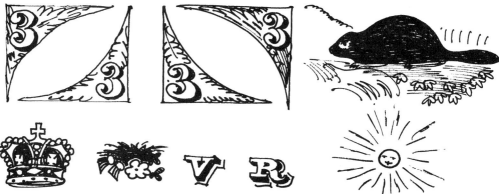

Postage stamps: portraits

The most usual feature on a stamp, apart
from the value or denomination, is a
portrait head; these examples, all enlarged
by the same amount, show how many ways
there are to reproduce even a simple
portrait. The two on the left show the
advantage the engraver has in working
from a conventional painted portrait (top),
rather than from a photograph, with its
uneasy informality (below).

The three portraits of Queen Victoria are
embossed, surface-printed, and line-
engraved; they present a strong contrast
between the idealized portrait convention
of the first two and the much more realistic
(as well as older) head in the third.
Although the surface-printed head was
very well-engraved (by Joubert de la
Ferté) and easy to print cheaply, it had
none of the tonal range of line-engraving.
This shows up well in the next three
portraits: a bust, a bust-like profile, and a
three-quarter view, all of great distinction.

The last three show how photography
brought new problems, but also opened
up completely new possibilities. The
Edward VIII photograph caused
difficulties in the treatment of the
background, due to the need to contrast
the light profile and the darkly-shadowed
hair. This danger was avoided in the
distinguished Dutch stamp, on which the
photograph is light enough all over to
appear as a simple light silhouette. The
Churchill head, although it might
superficially look like a boldly-massed
drawing, was in reality an unretouched
line print made from a detail of the
famous Karsh portrait.

Top:
Engraved stamp from painted portrait.
Engraved stamp from photograph.

Right:
Treatment of stamp portraits.

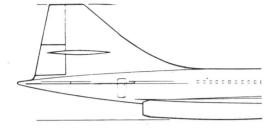

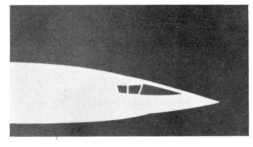

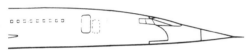

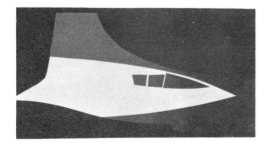

Postage stamps: designing is deciding

The first decision to take in designing
a stamp is one of subject matter, and
careful and imaginative research is the
essential first step. There is usually plenty
of interesting raw material and it can be
very difficult discarding 90 per cent of
this in order to concentrate on the rest.
I find it is useful to make small sketches
and jottings at stamp scale; as one grows
more confident in a promising idea it can
then be taken a step further, or dropped
before too much time and energy has been
spent on it. The Concorde design (left)
was very simple to carry out – silhouettes
of nose and tail taken from the
manufacturers' drawings and laid over
each other in contrasting colours – but
even simple ideas like this only seem to
develop gradually in the course of a job,
and seldom come as instant flashes of
inspiration at the outset.

It can be extremely hard to decide on the
best treatment. How should one portray
a ship? In perspective or in elevation?
At anchor or under full sail? In the water
or floating in air? Should one show the
complete hull, or only take it down to the
waterline, or isolate a significant detail
like a funnel or a figurehead? And should
it then be drawn, engraved, painted, or
cut out of film? In making sketches and
brief visual notes, one gradually finds out
what choices are available, which will
work best, which might make an
interesting set of designs, which are blind
alleys. It's a good idea to pin a sheet of
these jottings on the wall and look at them
afresh from time to time, to let one's views
about them grow unconsciously; it's a bad
idea to try to hurry this part of the work.

Left: Development of a stamp design.   Above: Preliminary sketches for stamp designs.

Actual stamp (this size)

Postage stamps: building a ship

When one is designing postage stamps, having settled on broad questions of design and treatment, it is then a different kind of task (sometimes an easier one) to carry the work out. The 'Great Britain' design was built up of a series of bits of coloured Letrafilm, each representing one printing colour. Very simple tone to suggest modelling was then sprayed on with an airbrush, and in some ways the work became rather like real shipbuilding. The hull was almost completed before the deck-houses and the funnel (prefabricated on a different drawing-board) were added; the lifeboats, masts, rigging, and the decorative gilded flourishes at the stem and the stern came last of all.

One has to do one's best to make use of the virtues of whatever printing process is being used; in this instance, photogravure could show the soft gradations of the modelling, and even the roundness of the masts, but the rigging had to be much simplified for this process. Offset-litho could have printed more detailed rigging, but would have been unable to cope so well with the tones of modelling on the hull.

A pictorial stamp and the elements that go to make up the design, in course of assembly.

Original artwork (actual size)

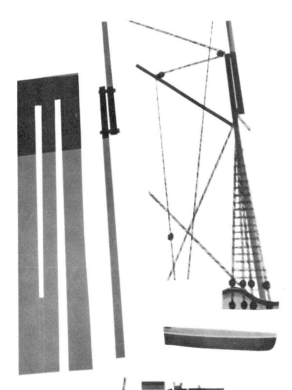

1. Outline of hull

2. Tone added to suggest modelling

3. Upper timbers scored

4. Windows taken out, rigging added.

Postage stamps: the outline of a stamp

It is easy to forget that, while a stamp is perforated in a rectangle, the design on it can be almost any shape, regular or quite irregular. These three ovals are all agreeable in their simplicity: indeed, it would be hard to better the plain fat-faced numbers on the Mexican ones. (Note how the mechanical patterning of the ellipse between the lettering and the inner oval varies in thickness, so that the latter does not become too long and thin in proportion.)

The cathedral designs (opposite) have a completely irregular outline. Gothic cathedrals have spiky silhouettes which stick out at awkward places; one of their great beauties is the intricacy of their details. On anything as small as a stamp the designer has to choose between showing the whole thing or concentrating on the significant or telling details – in this instance, the central tower of each cathedral. This made it possible to suggest the smaller-scale characteristics of an Early English tower or a Perpendicular Lantern, and also to suggest the powerful and creative constructive spirit at work in the stone.

Anglers are supposed to have a special feeling for the fish that get away from them, and I suspect that most designers have a similar affection for those designs which, like these, never got printed.

Right:
Projected designs for a series of stamps commemorating English cathedrals.

Top:
Coin treated for photography.

Above:
Coats of arms showing differing proportions.

Right:
Experimental sheet of stamps: the 'Rulers of Britain'.

Postage stamps: 'Rulers of Britain'

On a sheet of traditional line-engraved stamps each image is made by simply impressing the same roller die in a new position, so that every image is absolutely identical. The same principle applies in making offset or gravure plates from one negative by the 'step-and-repeat' process. But as photographic techniques have developed, a larger area can be repeated, and so there is no longer any technical need to repeat the *same* stamp right over a complete sheet, even if, in the meantime, Warhol has experimented with a repeated stamp-like image as an *aesthetic* device. The designs opposite form a section of a sheet of 'Rulers of Britain', produced as part of a commission from the Post Office to produce experimental designs. The portraits were prepared from a variety of originals, mostly from line prints of photographs of coins and sculpture. This produced the extreme tonal contrasts. The Edward VII head started as a penny, sprayed all over with matt black paint and then re-sprayed at a very low angle with white, to give the low-relief effect. The James II head originated in a photograph of the statue in Trafalgar Square. The coats of arms were chosen after examining innumerable possible versions, for their compact outline and legibility at small scale; a few of the other versions (at the left) show the extremes of proportion between upright and horizontal in which this familiar device may be found. Even at $\frac{3}{8}$ in. wide it remains unmistakable.

The complete sheet was proofed in a regular alternation of several related colours.

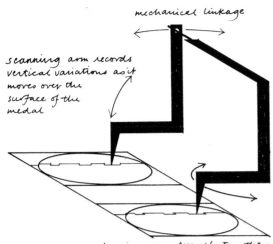

mechanical linkage

scanning arm records vertical variations as it moves over the surface of the medal

drawing arm translates these into horizontal variations as it moves over a plate and records an image.

Techniques of engraving: medal-engraving

The mid-nineteenth century was notable for its optimistic faith in the beneficial links becoming possible between art and science. A minor but interesting example of this is the medal-engraving machine: a device for translating a low-relief original (such as a medallion or ornamental plaque) into a flat linear image. The machine scans back and forth over the medallion in a series of close parallel lines, and every *vertical* movement caused by its uneven surface is transformed by a mechanical linkage into an identical *horizontal* quiver in the drawing arm, which is itself tracing a similar series of parallels, not unlike the lines on a television screen. The range of uses for this machine is limited, and by now it is hardly used except by security printers for portraits and background patterns. But some of its early products had a rather uncanny mechanical beauty, and gave a foretaste of photographic block-making long before this had actually developed. (An additional bizarre by-product was its ability, by pre-setting, to hugely exaggerate and distort the modelling it reproduced.) The examples (opposite), illustrate the finished medal-engraving and (below), the original from which it was produced. A further example with an enlarged detail for comparison appears overleaf. The detail shows the strange robot-like character of the line, foreshadowing the computer-controlled drawings familiar today.

Left:
The principle of medal-engraving.

Right:
Medal-engraved cartouche based on design at foot of page.

Seal of Queen Elizabeth I 1558. Produced by the
French engravers Henriquel Dupont for *The
Numismatical and Glyptical Cabinet, c.* 1825. Medal
engraved to the size shown here and detail (opposite)
enlarged to the same area to show technique of
contour engraving.

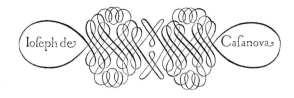

Techniques of engraving: engine-turning

An endless line has a strange visual fascination: where can the pen have started? Is there no hidden end tucked away in one of the clumps of complication? Casanova's devices (Madrid 1650) are simply pleasant patterns; but in London, at the same time, the writing master Edward Cocker had already taken the questionable step towards representation, hoping that:

> 'Some may be drawne, as I was, by
>   delight
> In apish ffancies, and so learne to
>   write.'

The mechanically-minded nineteenth century was alive to the new possibilities of such an endless line when it was created with the cold precision of mechanical engraving; and siderography, or 'engine-turning' on a 'rose-engine' became a highly-developed form of decoration. In circles or ovals it was excellent for framing portraits or illustrations, or the numerals on the increasingly numerous banknotes. It could be either linear and simple or endlessly lacy, with the delicate *moiré* effects caused when near-parallels cross each other at an angle.

Top left:
Writing master's exercise in a design from a continous line.

Middle:
A Queen's signature.

Left:
Edward Cocker, English writing master, using a continuous-line technique for decoration and illustration.

Right:
Specimen sheet from engine-turning engraver.

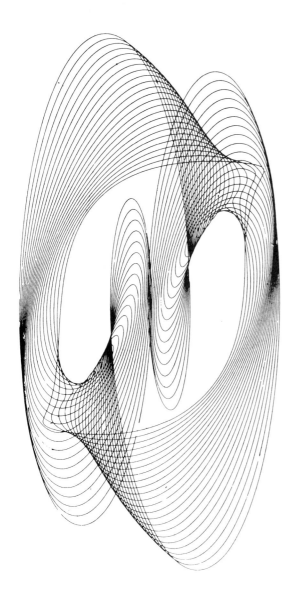

Techniques of engraving:
the harmonograph or pendulum machine

Mechanical turning of the basic sort on the previous page consists of the repetition of an identical device, moved on slightly each time but otherwise remaining quite unchanged. Later in the nineteenth century the invention of the 'harmonograph' took the idea a stage further; by linking a drawing-arm with a number of pendulums and setting the whole thing in motion, the arm would trace an irregular curve which was repeated each time through a slightly smaller orbit as the pendulums gradually sank to rest. (Hervey Benham of Colchester even constructed a two-colour harmonograph which, when seen through tinted glasses, produced a 3-D image.) Much more recently, the security printers De La Rue have produced a 'fantasy-lathe' which by a combination of pre-set gears can trace (and repeat at will) an infinite range of patterns with the delicate contrasts of the two examples shown here. These may be delightful objects in themselves, but their usual function is to provide areas of intricate decorative pattern like these examples. Because the formula for setting-up the lathe to produce the patterns can be simply noted down, the patterns can be chosen once for a particular purpose and then set up again as often as necessary, the formula becoming the client's own special property.

Above and right:
Designs from a pendulum machine.

De La Rue Co Ltd

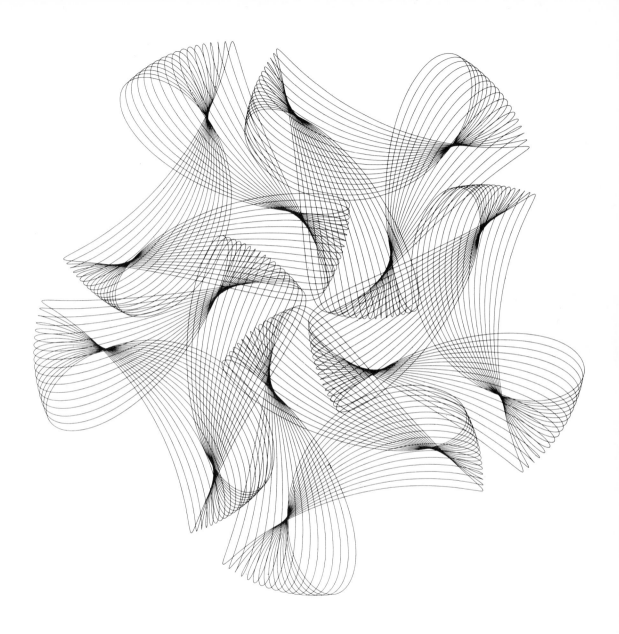

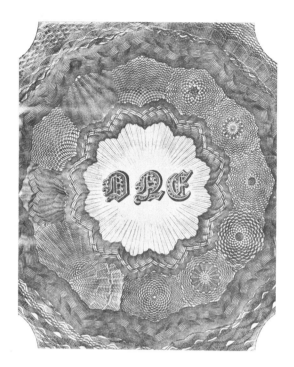

Banknote design

The two specimen banknotes opposite represent traditional design in this sphere at two extremes. The airy white spaces, simple script and realistic illustration of the Kington and Radnorshire Bank, with its conventional romantic ruin and its restrained and legible layout, contrasts strongly with the midland exuberance of the Huddersfield Banking Company, where the white paper is almost entirely covered by complicated pattern. (Oddly enough, there is more to look at or take pleasure in on the simpler design; one cannot look at repeated mechanical pattern for long with much interest.) Since the eighteenth century, banknote designs have gradually evolved from simple copperplate engravings in one colour on white paper to the multi-colour, multi-process printings in use nowadays. These changes have been hastened by the continual need to outwit hopeful forgers, and have been made possible by increased mechanization not only of printing but also of the design processes, so that nowadays much of the heavily overprinted pattern covering both surfaces of a banknote is mechanically created. This does not remove the designer's responsibility, but rather switches it to a different plane: to the tasteful massing of blocks of pattern and the harmonious arrangement of colour, decoration, lettering and illustrative engraving, to form a graceful whole.

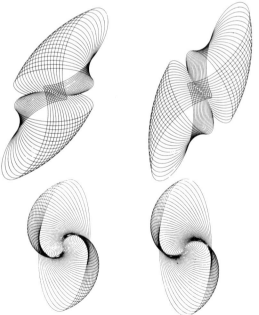

Examples of complicated engine-turning. *De La Rue Co Ltd*

Right:
A comparison of banknote designs.

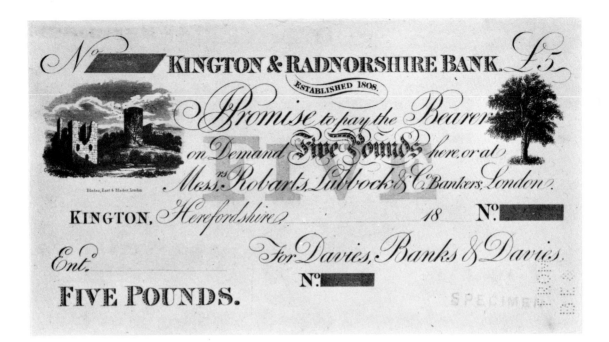

The banknote designer's problems have always centred on reconciling opposites: picture and value; type and cashier's signatures; the front and the back. The traditional solution was to weld the whole thing together with heavy and ornate borders and heavily-shadowed engraver's lettering: this made an excellent and workable, if very conventional, style, which still persists in many countries.

The Ecuador ten sucres note (opposite) is a good example of the genre. Sebastián de Benalcázar seems protected not only by his own full armour but by an inextricable tangle of complications, yet it can all be dismantled quite simply into its constituents. All are miniature designs in their own right: bank name; cashier's signature panel; denomination once in words and six times in figures (twelve if you count the tiny ones). Add a maze of intricate mechanical engraving and print in several colours and the result is a good chunk of the rich, traditional wedding-cake school of design, which is as heavily-encrusted and satisfying as an Edwardian merry-go-round.

This comparison extends even to the baroque heaviness and flowing curve of the main line of lettering, echoing another familiar fairground convention.

Although profuse and intricate decoration is hard to imitate by forgery, it is even harder to recapture the subtleties of expression of a face. Portraits have therefore remained a constant feature of security printing, achieving as time goes by almost mythical stature.

Above:
An analysis of banknote design.

Right:
Back and front of a traditional banknote still in use today.

Banknote design: a modern banknote

Attempts to break away from this
security-tradition printing have not
usually been very successful, lacking the
workmanlike conviction and
professionalism of the traditional notes.
But these Swiss banknotes are an
interesting mixture of traditional flourishes
and complexity with clean layout: richly
ornate numerals blend with areas of
sophisticated mechanical engraving, and
sensitive and expertly engraved
illustration.

Although the casual user would hardly
realize it, it is nowadays usual for a
banknote to be printed by a combination
of all the three main techniques of
letterpress, engraving or recess printing,
and offset-lithography. A rainbow-like
variety of colour can be added by varying
the colour fed on to the ink-rollers; a
method of printing known as split-duct,
because of the divisions in the ink trough.
It is possible to print simultaneously on
both sides of a sheet and still retain
perfect register, so that an apple tree on
the front (for instance) would fit perfectly
over the red apples printed on the back.
The complexity of all this makes it an
expensive business even to prepare to put
a banknote into production. A round
figure of £5000 has been quoted to cover
the costs of the initiation process, before
printing actually started. But no substitute
has yet been found which can entirely
replace the skill of the steel-engraver who
translates the tonal original into the
linear engraved picture.

Right:
Contemporary banknote design.

No. 286,—5s.

No. 289,—6s.

Design in miniature may be about small things, but I hope that this book has in some measure shown how much work and thought goes into the design of these coins, stamps and various devices. Just as Bewick on the surface of a small boxwood block could distil the essence of the Northumbrian countryside, so could the anonymous die-cutters of Greek and Roman times compress the spirit of their age on to the faces of a coin, and even in some small degree contribute to our understanding of that spirit. Queen Victoria was never so well served by her portrait painters as she was by the combined efforts that went to making the Penny Black; and, in this miniature form, she certainly grew familiar to many who knew no other image of her.

But compression of a visual idea into miniature terms is rather like condensing a complex thought into an epigram: to work successfully it must be selective and pared down to essentials. The process of reducing an idea or a design to its most basic form, discarding on the way the interesting but inessential details, is a fascinating exercise, but not a particularly simple one. All in all the fact that numerous more or less conflicting graphic elements, as well as the personal predilections of both designer and client, have to be resolved on such a small scale, does, to paraphrase Dr Johnson, indeed wonderfully concentrate the mind.

Left:
Stock blocks, Albion and Columbian printing presses.